IMAGES OF ENGLAND

NEW MILTON

IMAGES OF ENGLAND

NEW MILTON

MALCOLM BAILEY AND CATHERINE LAKE

TEMPUS

Frontispiece: The Pantiles, in Lymington Road, in the 1950s. The shops, from left to right, are: Mann Bros, A. Banks Tobacconist & Confectioner, L.A. Garman Knitting Wools and Mary's Café.

First published 2003

Tempus Publishing Limited
The Mill, Brimscombe Port,
Stroud, Gloucestershire, GL5 2QG

© Malcolm Bailey and Catherine Lake, 2003

The right of Malcolm Bailey and Catherine Lake to be identified as the Authors of this work has been asserted in accordance with the Copyrights, Designs and Patents Act 1988.

British Library Cataloguing in Publication Data.
A catalogue record for this book is available from the British Library.

ISBN 0 7524 3060 2

Typesetting and origination by Tempus Publishing Limited
Printed in Great Britain by Midway Colour Print, Wiltshire

Contents

Right: The water tower, from a postcard postmarked 1914. The water tower was built in mock Tudor style by the West Hants Water Co. in 1900 and a new rector, on arrival at the town, assumed that the tower was a Tudor castle! In the 1910 official guide of the Milton Ratepayers Association, the tower was described as 'a large and handsome octagonal water tower erected close to New Milton station, ensuring a high pressure both night and day'. Towards the end of the Second World War it is reported that a New Milton fireman jumped from the top of the tower in order to test a new type of safety blanket!

Below: The Milton Toilet Saloon in Station Road, owned by F. Dawes in the early 1930s, offered ladies' and gents' hairdressing, manicure and chiropody, as well as sunshades and umbrellas. The 'Saloon' part of the name was later changed to 'Salon'.

Introduction

If there is ever a prime example of a town that demonstrates all of the dramatic changes in society, the growth of commercial development and the modernisation of settlements, New Milton certainly has to be one of the best. Whilst it is actually quite young in its existence, at least in terms of its modern name and establishment as a town in its own right, it has expanded and evolved at a rapid pace throughout its centenary – which was celebrated back in 1996.

The town has certainly had its fair share of characters, personalities and pioneers, all of whom have played their own part in making New Milton the place it is today. The population has continued to grow in number as has the range of recreation facilities, from golf courses and holiday parks, to sports and arts centres. There are several beautiful churches in the area, in addition to a variety of pubs and social clubs – all adding to a thriving community atmosphere.

When you look at New Milton, with its eventful history and its fascinating pre-history, it is simply amazing just how much has occurred in such a small part of the British Isles. The village started out in life as a farm, in the middle of a number of other farms (the tons), and has grown in size and popularity as a small town in its own right – with many claims to fame!

The first book on fossils in Great Britain was written by Brander in 1766 on the subject of fossils found at Barton-on-Sea, where Bronze Age urns were later discovered from around 1910. Barton was also the location where an example of a very rare Celtic gold coin, thought to be from around 50 BC, was found! The first concrete bridge in the country was also built at Chewton Bunny just outside the town.

There are also many interesting stories of smuggling in and around the area. There was even a shipwreck lying on the beach at Barton once upon a time. New Milton has always had a strong link with its surroundings by several means of communication. The first significant link was its railway in 1888, placing Milton immediately on the main line, shifting the focus from the old village and creating a brand new centre of activity.

Next were the post offices which, thanks to Mrs Newhook and her decision to open a new sub-post office near the station around 1895, helped give Milton its 'new' name.

The town has all the services we have come to expect today in order to enjoy a good standard of living, the most basic of which is clearly epitomised by the Water Tower in Osbourne Road. Much like the tower in the neighbouring village, Sway, it is recognised as the leading landmark in the town nowadays. It is quite possibly the most photographed place in the area, has often been drawn and painted by passionate artists, and has also been used as the basis for a logo for the freshly re-formed New Milton & District Chamber of Commerce.

In the last decade, as technology has continued to take over our lives, the town was one of the first in the Forest area to be given a digital exchange and have ADSL (Broadband Internet Access) made available. The town also has full access to all the major mobile phone networks, although it remains one of few areas in the south without cable television at the time of writing. Well . . . you can't have everything!

The town of New Milton is now a popular centre for tourists and visitors to the area. To the north stretches the New Forest with its beautiful scenery, traditional dwellings and inhabiting wildlife that roams around the small villages there. To the east lies Lymington – an old town famous for its quay and facilities for sailing, in addition to its ferry port that runs regular crossings of the Solent, to Yarmouth on the Isle of Wight. The island can be seen to the south of Barton-on-Sea from the cliff-top. The Needles lighthouse is prominent as well, as is Hurst Castle and Hurst Spit leading to it. Also identifiable is Hengistbury Head, Swanage, the Purbeck Hills and – on a clear day – Weymouth.

New Milton has become a hive of activity over the last 100 years, now fulfilling a diverse range of needs for those who live and work in the town, from every type of shopping to a healthy range of recreational activities and pastimes. It enjoys its commemorative events, has a large number of hard-working committees and voluntary organisations within its boundaries, as well as a pro-active Town Council and equally supportive Youth Centre.

It is truly amazing just how many photographs exist, in residents' private albums and local business' offices, and we are extremely grateful to all those people who have kindly allowed us to share their photographs and postcards.

A great deal of thanks should also go to all those who have contributed to the compilation of this book, by way of the provision of historical data and the collaboration of information, not forgetting representatives from local media and press organisations.

We really hope you enjoy this book, and that it brings back many memories, especially if you once lived in New Milton or perhaps reside in the town now. If you are a youngster, you might not have even seen the area as it was 'back in the old days', but now you will know exactly what your family are talking about in those anecdotes and recitals!

one

Station Road North

Bank Terrace, as seen from the station entrance, c. 1904. The shops, from left to right, are: Matthews Watchmaker, Gore Hairdresser, W.E. Kirkman Cash Chemist, J.E. Hamblin, International Stores, A. Mintram General Draper & Milliner, Lloyds Bank. On the left, beyond the shops, the east side of Station Road was private housing beyond Osborne Road and largely remained so until the 1960s.

The Milton Hotel built, by Mr Hugh Wyeth, soon after the railway station was completed. He was a man of great foresight in building Milton Hall and a large house in Station Road. He also predicted that Milton would become a borough town. The hotel later became the Speckled Trout before its demolition to make way for the new health centre, pharmacy and convenience store that now stands there. Mr Hugh Wyeth died in 1900.

The Tea Gardens at the Milton Hotel, owned at this time by E.S.G. Harvell, from a postcard dated 22 April 1926.

Indian troops ready to leave New Milton railway station, to serve in the First World War, following their convalescence at Barton-on-Sea.

Station Road North, looking towards the town centre from the bridge, *c.* 1953. Alderson's radio and television shop (No. 4) was occupied by W.E. Kirkman from around 1910 until the 1940s to early 1950s, before they moved to No. 22 Station Road – adjacent to the Unionist Club. Pratt's furnishers, drapers and nursery specialists occupied the shop in 1955, followed later by A.R. Hawkes photographic gift shop in 1958.

Looking down Station Road North again, southwards, *c.* 1909. The nearest shop, on the right, is the shop and tearoom owned by Mr John Farwell's Milton & Manor Farm Dairies. Two doors away is Barrow's Dairy shop – one of Mr Farwell's main competitors. Mr Alfred Barrow owned the shop, the brother of Miss Alice Penn Barrow, who died in October 1934, aged sixty-six. During her farming life she first took over the running of Gore Farm on the death of her father, then bought Woodcock Farm (Hordle) in 1918, which she farmed for three years, as well as buying Downton Manor Farm. She was a staunch Nonconformist and an active Sunday school worker in the Methodist Church at Wootton. As well as her family, and many notable local business people, the Mayor of Christchurch – Alderman Norman Barnes – also attended her funeral. Barrow's Dairy was eventually incorporated into Milton & Manor Farm Dairies in 1931. The donkey cart, on the left, belongs to Ashley Post Office. It waits for mail to be collected from Edward Novelle's New Milton Post Office on the opposite corner.

Right: The staff of Misselbrook & Weston take time out to be photographed outside the shop, which stood next to the railway line on the west side of Station Road, in 1911. The two members of staff, second and third from the right of the group, are Bert Keeping and Fred Brewer. Fred was the step-grandson of Eli Corbin who built the shop. The New Milton branch of Misselbrook & Weston was just one of many shops, later becoming the M & W chain of convenience stores, now part of the much larger One Stop group.

Below: An advertisement in the 1910 official guide of the Milton Ratepayers Association for Archibald H. Skoyles, the first commercial occupant of the former Milton Hall. Cecil G. Foot, brother of Bevan H. Foot – a well-known local grocer – was the second occupant.

Milton Hall in a photograph, from an advertisement, in Cecil G. Foot's own 1939 guide. The shop was taken over later by Porter & Clark, a seed merchant, and has now become a carpet shop.

J.E. Hamblin of Bank Terrace was the first of several businesses operating as a newsagent, stationer and tobacconist at this location. This advertisement appeared in the 1910 Official Guide of the Milton Ratepayers Association.

The same shop, under the ownership of Joseph Wood Murray in this photograph, was first owned by J.E. Hamblin when Bank Terrace was built around 1903. By 1912, the shop had been sold to William Edward Pope, and many pieces of crested china appeared with the backstamp 'Made for W.E. Pope, The Library, New Milton', as were a wide range of local picture postcards. The next owner was J.W. Murray, and the shop continued under his ownership until 1954, when the business was purchased by brothers George and John Stickland. Around 1962, due to expansion, it was necessary to open another shop at the newly-built No. 98 Station Road. This shop was run by George Stickland and was named 'Stationery House', while John remained at the shop in Bank Terrace. In 1990, the shop was sold to Balfour, while Stationery House remained until 1993, when the business was sold to Hodgkinson's Stationers.

Station Road North, looking towards the station, around 1915. The original post office was opened here in 1895, by Mrs Emma Newhook, but moved to premises just north of the railway bridge to share the building occupied by Fred Keeping's cycle shop. Mrs Newhook was responsible for the town's present name, obtaining an agreement from the Civic Parish Council and the Lymington postal authorities, to call her post office 'New Milton Sub-Post Office' in 1896. The name New Milton was adopted for the station, originally called 'Milton for Milford-on-Sea', on 1 May 1897. Edward Novelle, trading as Novelle & Co., took over the post office in September 1901 and moved to the corner of Whitefield Road later that year. The business expanded to include cycles and repairs, an estate agency, tobacco, stationery and confectionery. The post office was run mainly by Mrs Novelle due to Edward's many commitments which included the Unionist Club, of which he was a founder member, and the parish council.

The Misses Mintram (right) in the doorway of their shop in Bank Terrace in the early 1930s. Standing next to them in the doorway is staff member Winifred Lightfoot.

Another photograph of Station Road North, looking towards Whitefield Road, *c.* 1903. To the right is Bank Terrace, where Wilts & Dorset Bank moved to in 1904 from the west side of the road, later changing to Lloyds Bank. The building on the other corner, occupied by Novelle & Co. in this photograph, later became The Wee Cake Shop (known in the 1970s as Patisserie Charles), owned by Mr and Mrs Charles. Subsequent business included P.J. Patisserie and La Poussin. In December 1987 one of the employees of La Poussin, Alan Selby, took over the business and Selby's Bakery traded here until 1996.

W. E. KIRKMAN,

Dispensing Pharmacist and Photographic Chemist.

Telephone No. 9.

High-class Modern Pharmacy.

Highest Quality.   Store Prices.
Oxygen always in stock.

LARGE STOCK OF

Photographic Apparatus.

Specialist in Developing Films and Plates.
Prompt Despatch.   Personal Attention.

Daily Deliveries to Barton-on-Sea, Highcliffe, Hordle,
Milford, Sway and Wootton.

5, BANK TERRACE, NEW MILTON
(Opposite the Station).

William Ernest Kirkman opened his first shop in 1906, at No. 5 Bank Terrace, and went on to open a total of eight shops in the borough. A 1933 advertisement lists branches in New Milton, Milton Green, Barton-on-Sea and Milford-on-Sea, as well as Highcliffe and Burley. He was a founder of the Ratepayers Association in 1910, founded the volunteer fire brigade and went on to become Mayor of Lymington Borough. Mr Kirkman retired in 1960 and died, in 1967, aged ninety-one.

New Milton.

Station Road in the 1910s. The shops, from left to right, are: Hilliar & Co. Cycle Agents; George Elliott Outfitters and Tailors; Parks & Co.'s New Milton Fruit Stores; White & Pitman Drapers and Milliners. The photograph shows the poor condition of the road and pavements in the years prior to the forming of New Milton Urban District Council in 1926.

White & Pitman,

GENERAL DRAPERS
✳ & MILLINERS ✳

Costumiers

LADIES' AND CHILDREN'S OUTFITTERS.

LONDON HOUSE,
New Milton, Hants.

Agents for **ACHILLE SERRE Ltd., Cleaners & Dyers**

White & Pitman were the first occupants of No. 14 Station Road, one of the newly-built shops south of Whitefield Road, in 1910. The premises were later occupied by Bon Marche drapers in the 1930s, Alderson's electrical store in the 1950s and Toys A'gogo in the 1970s.

Greengrocers' displays have changed very little over the years as this picture of Parks & Co.'s New Milton Fruit Stores shows.

George Elliott opened his first shop, the Lymington Clothing Mart, at No. 87 High Street, Lymington, on 19 April 1872. By 1910 there were branches in New Milton, Lymington, Lyndhurst, Brockenhurst and Freshwater, Isle of Wight and, later, Christchurch. The Lymington shop is still open today, and is run by George Elliott's great-granddaughter, Jenny.

The Milton Unionist Club, shown here in the early 1920s, was founded in 1911. A change of name to New Milton Conservative Club was proposed, and accepted unanimously, by members at the Annual General meeting on 26 February 1971. The photograph clearly shows the absence of any development to the south of the club.

Hugh Wyeth's house, on the corner of Station Road and Ashley Road, from a postcard dated 1905. The fields of Whitefield Farm are on the left. The message on the back reads 'This is our lodging at Milton'.

The Scala Cinema, originally an army hut in Christchurch, was erected in 1919. It bore the name Wescott & Wilkinson from 11 May 1921. The building later housed Miss L. Ashby's café and confectionery shop to one side and W.F. Marlow's shoe shop on the other. The cinema closed in 1929, with business transferred to the newly-built Waverley Cinema, although the Scala was used for stage performances for a few years before its demolition in 1934.

May 14? / 34

With Compliments from
THE SCALA CINEMA
NEW MILTON

Above: A photograph taken on 14 May 1934 during the demolition of the Scala Cinema. A parade of several shops was built on the site.

Left: A souvenir card from the Scala Cinema. Betty Blythe's film career started in 1918 and she was the star of films such as *The Queen of Sheba* (1921) and *She* (1925).

Smith & Son, at No. 74 Station Road with printing works behind, was founded in 1923 by Basil Smith. Interestingly, although Basil did not have a son at this stage, he added '& Son' to the name of the business, perhaps to add credibility to a new company (presumably with the future in mind too)! The business undertook general printing work including the initial few copies of the *New Milton Advertiser* in 1928; an unofficial railway timetable commissioned by the New Milton stationmaster; as well as street directories and posters for Cecil G. Foot, the auctioneer, surveyor and estate agent. The photograph shows Mr Smith, with his mother, standing outside their shop in the 1930s. In the left-hand window is a range of writing and drawing instruments, postcards and general stationery, whilst the right-hand window is devoted entirely to a large range of cigarettes and cigars. The shop closed in 1951 and was rented to Hancock & Craft until they moved in the 1960s.

Hancock & Craft, at No. 74 Station Road, in the 1950s. The business was started in 1951, by Brian Hancock and Ted Craft, although the partnership was not long lasting. A demonstration room and workshop, which was first opened in Old Milton Road in the 1960s, was later merged with the retail outlet when it relocated to No. 110 Station Road. Brian Hancock retired in 1989 and the business continued under new ownership, although retaining the name Hancock & Craft, until 1992. The draper, M.F. Hawker, occupies the adjacent shop – formerly owned by the Misses Loveless. It was rebuilt in ten weeks following its destruction in the 1940 bombing.

Here we are looking south. The Westminster Bank, which can be seen on the left, merged with the National Provincial Bank (on the opposite corner) to become National Westminster Bank in 1968. On the other corner is Pauley's café and confectionery shop.

Station Road North, looking north from the crossroads, back in the 1940s. Just visible on the left is Pearson, Cole & Shoreland, the estate agents later to become Pearson, Cole & Hemens. The next two shops belonged to the Misses M. & C.M. Loveless, drapers and ladies' outfitters, and later Hawkers. Mr Hugh Wyeth's house can be seen to the right of the picture.

Station Road North in the 1970s. The last of the private houses (including Mr Hugh Wyeth's), on the right-hand side of the photograph, still remain. The square building mid-picture is Hinton House, the offices of James Truman Moore, the solicitors – now demolished to make way for a residential and shopping development. The traffic lights were installed in 1966.

Although not a strategic target, such as the cities of Southampton and Portsmouth, New Milton had its share of tragedy during the war. On the evening of Friday, 23 August 1940, twenty-four bombs, a mixture of incendiaries and high explosives, were dropped by a lone Luftwaffe bomber. There were twenty-four people killed, including nineteen civilians. The shops, from left to right, are: French Cleaning & Dyeing Co. (No. 72), Goodies (confectioner) (No. 70), Hewitt & Co (estate agents) (No. 68). The worst damage occurred at the drapers and ladies' outfitters shop of the Misses Loveless (No. 76), which was completely destroyed, and the neighbouring shop (previously the National & Provincial Bank) that was blown away. It was reported in the *New Milton Advertiser* at the time that the bomber circled the area for around half an hour before the bombs dropped. The paper reports, 'There is some criticism that the siren was not sounded, but this does not rest with the Local Authorities'. Could lives have been saved if the alarm had been raised? The bomber was chased westward into cloud by Spitfires, machine-gun fire was heard, then the raider was reported to have been shot down. Among the fatalities were the owner of Matthews' cycle shop, Lou Matthews, and a seventeen-year-old girl – Barbara Green – who had gone there to collect her bicycle. Most of the deaths were among those who were outside in the street at the time. The *New Milton Advertiser* reports, 'The raid afforded a very important object lesson to the public, of which they should take note. It is that the majority of those killed were in the street or out of doors . . . Be warned, therefore, get under cover of some sort directly you think there is a raider overhead'.

Above: An unidentified private house, on the east side of Station Road, was one of several which suffered extensive damage. In another bombing (on 8 August 1942) the owner of a bungalow in Spencer Road, and a soldier's wife and four young children living in Vincent Road were also killed.

Right: The worst of the bomb damage in New Milton totally destroyed the Misses Loveless' shop. Amazingly, nobody in the shop was killed; five girls survived by sheltering under a counter. The flat above the neighbouring shop was vacant at the time as the occupants, a mother and two children, had gone out.

The Cash Boot Stores (No. 62) and L.F. Matthews (No. 60) also suffered extensive damage.

Around the corner, in Old Milton Road, the builders' merchants' yard of Roberts Adlard received a direct hit. Fortunately they were closed at the time and nobody was on the premises. However, nine people were killed by another bomb in the road outside, splinters from which made a clean hole through the steel plate casing of a nearby electrical transformer. Roberts Adlard announced, in the *New Milton Advertiser*, that they were open again for business just two weeks later despite extensive damage.

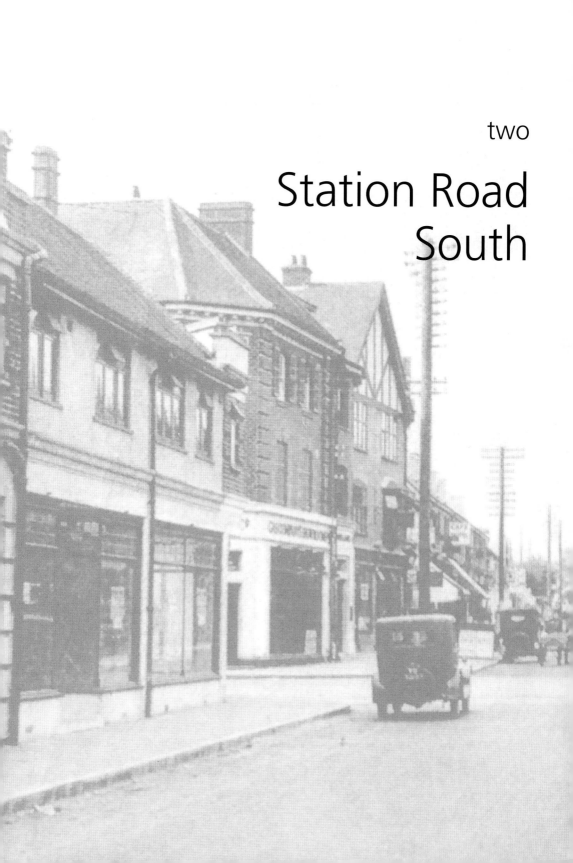

two

Station Road South

The Rydal Hotel, shown here in the 1960s, had the distinction of having Britain's oldest landlady – Gladys Walker. (Reproduced courtesy of St Barbe Museum, Lymington)

Looking towards the crossroads from Station Road South. The shop on the left is New Milton Pharmacies Ltd (W.S. Stephenson), with the Bournemouth Gas & Water Co. showroom on the far corner, whilst the two shops in between appear to be empty. The delivery bicycle seen in the middle of the road might well have belonged to The Beehive bakery. Their shop started off on the east side of the road and then moved across to No. 104.

H.S. Culver & Son's ironmongery shop just before its closure in 1995. The business was started in 1930 by Harold Culver, who had previously been an apprentice for five years with Chilvers, the ironmongers in Ringwood. His son, Tony, joined the business in 1943 and the business acquired its first delivery van at that time – a new Bedford bought for £160. Tony took over the business in 1980 when his father retired.

New Milton's main post office was built in 1933, the first official postmaster being Mr Weston, and the telephone exchange was installed upstairs in 1934. There were three full-time female telephone operators, plus a part-time seasonal operator, and there was a bedroom in the exchange for a male night operator. There were just six telephone subscribers in 1905. That had risen to 600 by 1933. By 1955, the main post office area encompassed Ashley; Barton-on-Sea; Bashley; Milford-on-Sea; Sea Road (Barton) and Wootton. The sub-post offices at Manor Road and Beechwood had been added by the 1960s. Its closure in 1995 was not without incident; compensation was awarded to staff due to the lack of proper consultation procedures prior to the relocation of the post office to Martins' newsagents on the east side of Station Road.

Station Road South in the 1950s. From the left are: H.S. Culver & Son's hardware store; Neville Hands' Greengrocery; J.H. Dewhurst Ltd Butchers; Nicholson's Radio & Television; R.H. Fagan Menswear; Boots Cash Chemists (later to move across the road adjacent to the crossroads); The Beehive (café, bakery and cake shop, owned by sisters Amy, Mabel and Violet Haynes); World's Stores (grocers and provision merchants); Croll (sports goods, toys and stationery). The shop occupied by Croll can be seen in the previous photograph as belonging to Moody's furniture store and removals company. The empty plot seen this side of it was later to be built on and occupied by Stationery House.

The single-storey shops to the east side of Station Road originally had their own service road before the widening of the high street. From right to left are: Hull & Henderson; Jill Petley; S.H. Petley & Co; Hull & Henderson's second office. This photograph was taken just prior to their demolition to make way for the retail development which includes Safeway supermarket.

The estate agents H.P. Hull, later to become Hull & Henderson, had an unusual miniature house outside their premises in the 1940s.

Station Road South around 1960. In the distance, on the right-hand side, the photograph shows shops set back from the road and later shops on the near right. An empty plot alongside the Midland Bank was where Fine Fare was built in 1961. The small shops, on the far side of the bank, were soon to be demolished. They included: Hull & Henderson (estate and travel agents, H.P. Hull in 1934); Jill Petley (stationer and bookseller); S.H. Petley & Co. (coal merchants); James O. Waite (chiropodist); Reeds Footwear & Repairs; as well as Westminster Bank on the south-east corner of the crossroads, later to merge with National Provincial Bank on the opposite corner, to become National Westminster Bank. The newer shops to the right of the picture are part of Westcroft Chambers and were built between 1955 and 1958. From the far end are: F.W. Woolworth; an unoccupied shop; Wilkins Bakery; Harlequin Café; another unoccupied shop; Westcroft Cleaners; Fox & Sons Estate Agents; then in the chambers, Harold G. Walker Solicitors. On a postcard from 1961, the manageress of Wilkins Bakery writes, 'Note the pretty little gardens in front of each shop, they are all in bloom now and look very pretty'.

Reg Fagan (right), who started the gents' outfitters at No. 108 Station Road in 1951, with his wife Gladys and manager Peter Roberts. Reg had previously worked for Bobbies and Robert Old, in Bournemouth, before starting his family business in New Milton.

Reg Fagan's son Robert started work in the shop in 1963 and took over the running of it when Reg died in 1989.

The Waverley Cinema was built on the south side of the town and opened on Tuesday,
5 November 1929 following the closure of the Scala Cinema. The *New Milton Advertiser* reported
at the time that the proprietor, Mr Haywood, 'seems to be of a somewhat retiring nature, for
there was not the "big drum" activity that one usually finds on such occasions'. The opening
programme consisted of a Pathé Gazette, Harold Lloyd in *Number Please*, Greta Garbo in *Love* and
an animal picture – *Dog Heaven* – which was a last-minute addition to entertain the children
present. The Waverley Orchestra, directed by Mr Reuben Price, played in the interval and was
well received. Mr Haywood's son, Cyril, joined the business in 1935 and took over from his
father when he joined the Navy at the beginning of the Second World War.

The Waverley Cinema closed its doors for the last time on Sunday, 17 September 1972 – the
final film to be shown was *Those Magnificent Men in Their Flying Machines*. The cinema was
demolished to make way for sheltered housing flats. These adverts from the *New Milton Advertiser*,
dated 16 September 1972, advertised the showing of the final film and announced the
continuation and relocation of Jack Plank's travel business.

Children photographed outside of the Waverley on a Saturday morning in the late 1940s or early 1950s. Like many cinemas, the Waverley held matinées on Saturday mornings, when the behaviour of the children was frequently bad enough for the performance to be stopped, and the manager would climb onto the stage and threaten that the cinema would be closed and they would all be sent home unless they behaved!

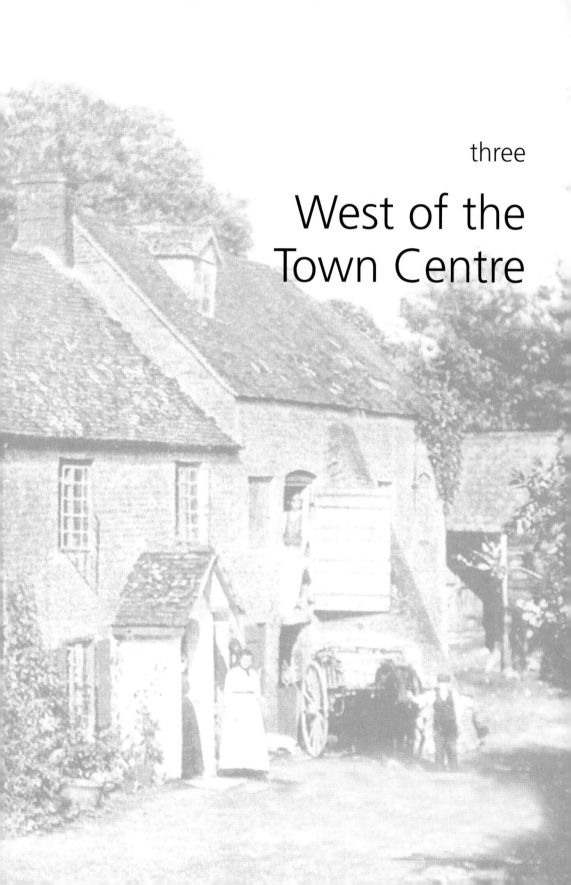

three

West of the
Town Centre

Wilfred Horsford, family butcher, standing outside his shop at No. 3 Old Milton Road. The shop was later bought by the aptly named Mr P.R. Bull and continued under that name with a succession of owners.

Opposite below: The yard of builders' merchants Roberts Adlard & Co. Ltd, situated in Old Milton Road on the original site of Hayward's farm, in the 1920s. This photograph shows the original farmhouse. The building was replaced with a purpose-built showroom and offices in 1935, but suffered a direct hit when the bombing took place on Friday, 23 August 1940. The building was rebuilt and continued until, in May 1988, it was demolished and replaced with shops and flats.

RECREATION GROUND AND MEMORIAL, NEW MILTON.

The war memorial in New Milton's recreation ground in 1937. The land was originally part of Hayward's farm in an area known as Whitefield. Public subscriptions totalling £850 were raised, mainly through the efforts of the rector, Reverend John Kelsall, allowing the recreation ground to open in 1920. The land for the bowling greens and tennis courts was donated by Bournemouth chemist, Mr Matterson, who lived in Fernhill Lane.

Leonard Hodges' greengrocery and floristry shop at No. 121 Old Milton Road, pictured here around 1948, was well known for specialising in fruits that were considered exotic at the time, such as melons, peaches and aubergines. Leonard William Hodges was born in Southampton and lived for a time in Plymouth. He then moved to New Milton to open his shop when the new parade in Old Milton Road was built in 1947. The floristry side of the business concentrated on making high-class bouquets for special events, as well as for funerals, under the supervision of Miss Shave. Leonard Hodges closed his grocery business in 1957, going on to run a public house in Wiltshire.

George Mentor's butcher's shop in Old Milton Road which, by 1934, had become J. Bugler. This was the only shop on the plot at the time the photograph was taken, but it was soon developed to become a parade known as The Terrace.

Left: New Milton Fire Station in Gore Road in the 1940s. The fire brigade was formed in 1912, although Milton Parish Council first purchased eight fire extinguishers in 1910, which were kept in various shops in New Milton, Ashley, Old Milton and Bashley. The brigade initially used a hand pump, with a 600ft hose that had to be taken to fires in the first available vehicle, which quite often turned out to be Mr Kirkman's sidecar. In 1929, the Parish Council purchased a Dennis fire appliance, and the brigade was called by means of mortar maroons being set off. The fire station was built in 1934, on the site of the former New Milton Urban District Council yard and the New Milton Motor Cycle Depot, and was demolished in 1974 when the present-day fire station was erected on the corner of Whitefield Road.

Below: New Milton's fire brigade, pictured here, on Sunday, 3 September 1939 – the day that the Second World War broke out. The policy during the war was to have up to 300 firemen on call to deal with fires in Southampton and Bournemouth following heavy bombing raids. These men lived in New Milton temporarily, having been drafted in from quieter areas, and were moved around the country as necessary.

Above: Lush Signs' Austin pickup, ready for a carnival in the early 1960s, with Jim's daughter Geraldine at the wheel.

Opposite above: Jim Lush's sign-writing career started as an apprentice to Don Burrey, who worked from his home, 'Arlesdene' in Old Milton Road. At this time, Jim was preparing sign boards and would be sent out to prime and paint shop fascias in preparation for sign-writing, which was carried out by Don. Following the development of Station Road by W.J. Keeping, from the Unionist Club southwards, all the shops were sign-written in this way by Don Burrey.

Opposite below: Jim Lush left in 1939 to start his own business from 'Glendevon', his home in Hobart Road, when Don Burrey joined the Army at the outbreak of the Second World War. Jim also joined the Army and was forced to wait until his return in 1946 to continue his business. In 1942, he married Maisie Mogg, whose family ran the nursery/seedsmen business F. Mogg & Sons in Hordle and Milford-on-Sea. The photograph shows Lush Signs' premises in Old Milton Road from 1952 until the present day.

Lush Signs' staff members photographed whilst working on-site near Lymington River in the 1960s. Brian Shores is on the right with Alf Pritchard nearest to the windscreen – the name of the young 'driver' of the Commer Cob van is not known.

Some of Lush Signs' more unusual sign-writing jobs:

Above: Commer horsebox for Merrie Stud of Wootton.

Above right: Mobile workshop for B.W.A. Russell of Oakwood Avenue, New Milton.

Right: Foden steam wagon restored by and sign-written for the Montagu Motor Museum, now the National Motor Museum in Beaulieu.

Left: The driver of New Milton Laundry's Morrison Electricar delivery van poses proudly beside his vehicle pictured here outside their Gore Road premises. New Milton Laundry ceased to trade on 31 December 1978 when it was taken over by Advance Laundries Ltd. (Photograph reproduced courtesy of St Barbe Museum, Lymington)

Below: Jim Jose purchased his bakery business, which included one delivery vehicle, from Mr W.M. Wilcox in 1945. Jim's son David joined the business in 1967 and expansion continued with the acquisition of several other businesses, including G.T. Tanner's Bakery of Boscombe, Gerald's Bakery of Bournemouth, Milford Bakery and the Hordle bakery of Frank Holes. By the time Jim died in 1977, the business had eleven shops, thirty vehicles and a staff of 150.

A Fordson van belonging to fishmonger W. Jones Ltd, whose shop was opposite Crossmead Avenue in Old Milton Road.

Cottages in Old Milton Road. From left to right are: S. Hunt (No. 1), A. Peckham (No. 2 – Thatch Cottage), S. Compton (No. 3 – Dawson Cottage), E. Dodge (No. 4 – Fern Cottage), H.T. Sherred (No. 5).

An aerial photograph of Naish Farm in the early 1950s, with Parkland Caravan Park in the distance.

A postcard, postmarked 1960, showing views of Naish Farm Holiday Camp.

These bungalows on the cliff-top at Naish Farm Holiday Camp have long since vanished over the edge due to erosion.

Opposite below: The bridge and waterfall at Chewton. Built in 1901, Chewton Bridge has the distinction of being the first reinforced concrete example in the country.

Chewton Bunny, shown here in the 1930s, had a reputation as a smugglers' landing place in the nineteenth century. This led to the building of a coastguard station at Barton-on-Sea with the Coastguard Cottages, built in 1868 – a lasting legacy of this time. The nearby house, Windyridge, now a nursing home, was the chief officer's house.

A postcard, addressed to John Farwell (see the chapter on Old Milton) and postmarked 1905, showing the Mill House at Chewton Glen.

The stream crossing between New Milton and Walkford showing the hazardous conditions experienced by travellers before hard road surfacing. The bend was later bypassed with the straightening of the road although it still exists as a service road.

four

Old Milton

Edward Chipperfield's grocery and drapery store to the north of Milton Green, Old Milton, with his 'lad' posing with the hand-propelled delivery cart.

The National Schools for infants and juniors, built in 1835 by the Church of England National Society. The schools moved to wartime huts at the east end of Gore Road just after the First World War, and the old school building was used by the Council until 1931.

A crowd listening to a brass band on Milton Green on Hospital Sunday, *c.* 1920. The surface of the Green was, at this time, mostly sandy soil rather than grass which indicates that it was a popular location for village gatherings. Edward Chipperfield's grocery and drapery store can be seen on the right, with the Wheatsheaf Hotel and A. Joy's sub-post office beyond.

A photograph taken in 1983, showing John Jordan's shop, originally owned by George Topp & Sons, and later Stanley Rushford, all butchers. The original shop was cob-built. In the background is the Poor House undergoing conversion to housing, and just visible on the right is Cook & Sons' engineering company, formerly a brass foundry belonging to John Adams.

The same view in March 1990 showing Jordan's just prior to demolition. The building to the right is Fusee House, named after the fusee chain manufacturing that took place in the Poor House, with Jordan House yet to be built next door.

Cook & Sons, whose Bedford CA van is shown here, occupied the former brass foundry on the junction of Lymington Road and Old Milton Road. The business was purchased around 1919 from John Adams by John Cook and his son Walter who were later joined by Walter's son Tony. Their main business was general engineering and repairing agricultural equipment, although they would undertake many different types of work, such as building horse-drawn milk floats, based on the Ford 8 chassis, for Hygienic Dairy. They later became well known as lawnmower engineers until the business finally closed in 1982.

A 1906-10 photograph of the horse-drawn delivery van belonging to Charles Peckham, the well-known baker at Milton Green. The driver is Charles' brother George Peckham.

Village Green, Old Milton, 1921. On the far left of the photograph can be seen the bakery and outhouse, next to the shop belonging to Mr George Peckham, who was also a grocer and mealman. The shop and adjoining house, with their distinctive chequered brickwork, were built in 1854 by his father Charles Peckham. On the right of the photograph, the white house later became a chemist shop and the thatched cottage was to be demolished and was replaced by a hardware store.

R. 195.—LYMINGTON[x] to Poole.

	M	F	M	F
to Downton[x]	—	—	4	—
Ashley Bridge	—	3	4	3
Cross Avon Water.				
Milton Green	2	—	6	3
Chuton Bridge[x]	1	—	7	3
bpCHRISTCHURCH[x]	4	—	11	3
Cross the Avon R.				
On r. to Ringwood, 7½ M.				
Iford Bridge[x]	2	1	13	4
Cross the Stour R.				
Bourne House	3	—	16	4
Parkson *Dorset*	4	—	20	4
bpPOOLE	2	—	22	4

Left: This table of fares, taken from the 1815 sixth edition of *The Great Roads of Britain* by John Cary, shows that the coach from Lymington to Poole stopped at Milton Green.

St Mary Magdalene's Church. The first church in the village of Milton was built in the thirteenth century, lasting until around 1830, when it was rebuilt with only the seventeenth-century tower remaining from the original building. Apart from some alterations, including the relocation of the main entrance to the tower on the west side and the addition of the church's distinctive lych gate, the building remains the same to the present day. Milton Parish Church has two sister churches – St Peter's in Ashley and St John The Baptist's in Bashley – and is part of the Anglican Diocese of Winchester, as well as being a parish within the Deanery of Christchurch.

Above: Milton Village around 1915, showing the Wheatsheaf Hotel and the George Hotel. The George was a thatched pub until 1905, when the present building was erected in its place. The Wheatsheaf has changed very little; a sub-post office originally stood next to the Wheatsheaf where the car park is now. The horse-drawn tanker is delivering Homelight paraffin outside Edward Chipperfield's grocery and drapery store.

Right: A lad with the delivery bicycle belonging to Kemsley & Son, The Stores, Milton. Originally Edward Chipperfield's grocery and drapery store, the shop was purchased by Mr Kemsley in 1919, and was later owned by Mr Britnell, then by Mr C.E. Robinson in 1934.

KEMSLEY & SON.
The Stores,
Milton.

The shops at Old Milton in the early twentieth century. The post office, founded on 14 July 1834, is on the left; at the time of this photograph, it was run by the Brownen family. One of the first postmasters, in 1855, was Edward Hayward who was also the local registrar and tax collector. His successor, Edmund Brownen, further extended his duties, not only as registrar, but also as the rate collector, vaccination officer and sanitary inspector. He was succeeded by his wife, Jane Brownen, in September 1899. The sign over the window reads, 'AM Brownen, Licensed to sell Tobacco'. The post office was later taken over by Mrs Agnes Joy, a daughter of the Brownen family, and the business was also advertised as a 'Registry Office for Servants, etc.', 'Cycle Agent & Repairer', 'Stationery & Fancy Goods', 'Cigarettes' and 'Fancy Goods'. The post office was demolished around 1950 to make way for the Wheatsheaf Hotel's new car park.

When the old post office closed, it was moved across the road to Mr R. Church's shop, where it remained until the 1990s, before moving next door into shops formerly occupied by Fulford's Dairy and A. Bennett, which have now merged to become a convenience store.

The story of Edgar's Dairies starts in 1888, when Mr John Farwell moved to New Milton from Dorset to rent Church Farm from Mr Merdin Radford, and also to marry Elizabeth Burry of Christchurch. The farm had a herd of eight cows and a milk round was started with one cart; the business soon started to grow with the coming of the railway that year. John Farwell was helped in the business by his three daughters, Grace, Evelyn and Dorothy. The latter married Fred Edgar in 1919. Fred and Dorothy managed Walkford Farm, which John Farwell had rented since 1900, and ran his farming and cheese-making business. Aubrey Farm, at Keyhaven, was purchased and a milk round was established in Milford-on-Sea. The retail business was divided in 1929, with Fred and Dorothy Edgar taking over the Milford-on-Sea area, and Jonathon and Evelyn (one of John's daughters) Fawcett taking over the New Milton operation. The businesses became known as F & D Edgar and Milton & Manor Farm Dairies respectively. The shop and café in Station Road was acquired around this time. The year 1934 saw the sudden death of Fred Edgar in Glasgow whilst he and Dorothy were taking their first holiday since they married.

The tenancy of Vidle Van Farm at Keyhaven was taken on in 1939 and, in May of that year, Dorothy's son John became a pupil of Mr Tom Parker in Fareham, returning in 1941 to help his mother with the family business. The year 1946 saw a major change in policy with the re-amalgamation of the two businesses and centralisation at Church Farm. In 1949 the name of the dairy was changed from Milton & Manor Farm Dairies to Edgar's Dairies Ltd, and some local businesses were acquired, including Aldridge's Dairies at Lymington and Lea Green Farm Dairy at Downton. At this time, Edgar's Dairies had retail shops at Lymington and Milford-on-Sea, as well as a sales counter at the dairy in New Milton.

Left: The 1950s saw the marriage of John Edgar to Angela Green as well as the formation of Edgar's Orange Drinks Ltd and the acquisition of more local dairy businesses. In 1961, Edgar's bought out the second largest dairy in the area, Hygienic Dairy in Ashley Road which, at that time, was bottling 800 gallons of milk a day, with thirteen milk rounds. Edgar's Dairies celebrated their centenary in 1988 although, sadly, John Edgar had died in 1970. The dairy was sold to Avonmore Foods (UK) Ltd in August 1993, and the Edgar's Dairies name was finally dropped in January 1994.

Below: On 12 June 1961 Edgar's Dairies, in association with the recently acquired Hygienic Dairy, opened a Mace grocery and dairy shop in the premises that was originally the late Evelyn Fawcett's shop.

Right: Edgar's Dairies roundsman Wilf Simpkins, with 'Charlie' pulling a horse-drawn milk float, on 24 July 1958. Wilf joined Edgar's in 1956 and rose to the position of manager before retiring on 31 March 1993, aged sixty-three. Horses were used to pull milk floats until February 1964, when 'Patch', 'Alice' and 'Darkie' were pensioned off.

Below: A horse-drawn milk float belonging to Fulford & Son, Milton Green Dairy. The dairy business was started in October 1933 by Mr Alex Fulford in the shop that he rented at No. 3 Milton Green, Old Milton, selling Channel Island milk, cream and other provisions. Fulford's milk became so popular that he started bottling milk on the premises, in buildings to the rear of the shop, and within a few months had commenced deliveries in the area. Several smaller dairies were acquired, including those of Davis in Gore Road, Don Sherred of Bashley Cross Road, and eventually all of the small dairies in Bransgore. Fulford's Dairy expanded to eight rounds, eventually delivering to many hotels and schools as well as to domestic customers, and delivering as far afield as Holmesley Aerodrome. As was the case with many other local dairies, the business was sold to Edgar's Dairies in May 1974.

PARKLAND, NEW MILTON, HANTS.

C.M.918

An aerial photograph of Parkland Caravan Park showing the large canteen and general store at the top of the picture. Christchurch Road can be seen at the bottom left with Top's Café, named after the owner G. Topham, between the caravan site and the row of terraced houses. The houses to the right are those of Chiltern Drive, the first phase of the residential development that was to envelop Parkland.

PARKLAND
CHRISTCHURCH ROAD, BARTON-ON-SEA
NEW MILTON

An advertisement for Parkland Caravan Park from the Borough of Lymington Guide of 1948/49.

" THE CARAVANNERS' PARADISE "

One of the original small shops at Parkland Caravan Park, run by Hygienic Dairy. The small shops were demolished later in the 1950s when a larger general store was built.

Leonard Hodges, in 1953, standing outside the greengrocery shop that he built himself at Parkland Caravan Park.

Houses and shops in Christchurch Road, opposite Fawcett Field, which is now the home of New Milton & Lymington Football Club. The shop to the right of the photograph was a general store which was owned by the Misses Elizabeth and Lucy Shave in the early 1900s, and was taken over in the 1930s by Mary Elizabeth Shave, before later reverting to a private house.

Shoemaker Alf Waterman outside his premises at No. 8 The Terrace, Old Christchurch Road, 1916-18. The shop was owned by Ben Plumley who lived with his family above the shop. Mrs Plumley let the front room shop to Alf because he had served in Siberia in the First World War and his pay was a year late in arriving.

five

Barton-on-Sea

Barton Court Avenue in 1921, showing the Indian Monument in the centre, with the Dome Hotel, built in the early 1900s on the left and Barton Court in the distance.

Above: An enlargement from the estate agent's booklet on the right, showing the non-existent pier and frontage. It is not known whether this was a proposed development or simply the product of an over-active imagination! The pier was erased from the picture in later editions of the booklet.

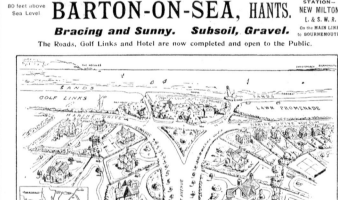

Above right: The cover of an estate agent's booklet produced in 1904, showing the layout of Barton-on-Sea after the Barton Court estate had been split up in the 1890s, with the development that had taken place since then. A rather fanciful addition to the scene is the pier and frontage just to the right of Barton Court (see enlargement above).

The Barton-on-Sea estate office.

Advertisements for businesses in the area, printed on the reverse of the estate agent's booklet.

Barton Court during the First World War, when Indian troops were sent to Barton-on-Sea for convalescence, initially at Mrs White's Barton Court Hotel then, as their numbers grew, in the specially built huts seen here on the right of the photograph.

Barton Court from the south-west in 1917, showing the convalescents' huts that were built in the grounds.

Barton-on-Sea Indian Memorial, from a postcard postmarked 1934. The Indian Memorial is one of only two Indian memorials in the country, the other being in Brighton. It was originally thought that both were built at the same time, although it has since been discovered that the one in Brighton was built later, in 1921. The Barton-on-Sea memorial, built in 1917, is the only one built before the war ended, and is the oldest memorial of the First World War in the country.

The unveiling ceremony of the Indian Memorial in 1917. All the officers and men appear to be in British uniform, so either the Indian troops were not invited or had left by this time.

The approach to Barton Court from Marine Drive West in 1917. The huts for the Indian troops can be seen to the left and right, and the Grand Marine Hotel, used as an overflow for Barton Court, is visible in the distance.

Above: Volunteers bathing at Barton-on-Sea in 1902. It looks like an overcast day, and if the number of men not bathing is anything to go by, it is not too warm either!

Opposite above: Entertainers from a 'Whizz Bangs' concert in 1917. Front row: Captain T.E. Gordon (left), Corporal Plenty (right). Middle row: Mrs W (centre), Private Johnson (right).

Opposite below: Another photograph of the 'Whizz Bangs' entertainers, with some of the concert organisers.

Marine Drive, Barton-on-Sea, around 1945. The little petrol forecourt was selling Shell and National petrol at this time. According to the clock over the butcher's shop of Barton & Co., it is 5 o'clock in the afternoon, and holidaymakers are returning from the beach to their hotels and guest houses for tea or dinner. To the left of the butcher's shop is the sub-post office. Barton-on-Sea's first post office was short-lived, opening on 17 March 1911 with Zoe Marion Furneaux as the postmistress, and closing again on 2 September 1911 when she resigned. It was not until 1 July 1925 that Barton again had a post office, this time under the management of William Gauld. Subsequent postmasters included Henry Harper on 1 April 1928; Phillip Henry Holdsworth on 1 February 1931; Frank Robertson Gulland on 1 February 1934 and Thomas Leslie Wakeford on 16 August 1946. There is still a post office at this location today.

Shops at Cliff Terrace, originally part of Barton Court, in the late 1940s. From left to right are: Ventana Hotel, Willis & Son South Hants Stores, Gullands Post Office, J.V. Winwood, W.E. Kirkman Chemist.

The tea garden of Barton-on-Sea's Cliff Café. The long garden became a crazy golf course before becoming a victim of the cliff erosion in later years. (Photograph reproduced courtesy of St Barbe Museum, Lymington)

The interior of Cliff Café in the 1920s.

Barton cliffs in 1905 were a popular destination for holiday makers and convalescents alike. Barton-on-Sea is renowned for its invigorating breeze, after which the First World War troops' magazine *Barton Breezes* was named.

A view of Barton Court, showing the extent of the erosion which continuously undermines the cliffs. Ongoing attempts to stop the erosion include groynes jutting out into the sea and the addition of piles and stone. All that remains of Barton Court is the northernmost wing, now called Cliff Terrace, the rest having been demolished due to erosion.

The shelter on Barton-on-Sea cliff-top in the 1950s, with the Grand Marine Hotel visible to the right, and the Tea Rooms to the far left.

The Marine Hotel undergoing alterations to make two buildings into one to act as overflow accommodation for Barton Court, *c.* 1910. On the far left is Alexander Plumley, a bricklayer and roofer, who also worked on New Milton's water tower in 1900. He was said to be the only man brave enough to climb onto the roof to erect the large chimney pots. He sadly died in 1943 when he fell off a roof and broke his neck.

The Grand Marine Hotel on Marine Drive East temporarily housed convalescing Indian and British soldiers during the First World War. The hotel closed in the 1960s and was sold to the Countrywide Holidays Association, who changed the name to Barton Chase, although the Marine Bar next door retained its name. The building was later demolished and was replaced by a block of flats.

GRAND MARINE HOTEL, BARTON-ON-SEA, NEW MILTON, HANTS.

Resident Proprietor :   2½ hours from Waterloo (Southern Rly).   Phone 25 New Milton.
A. S. CLARKE.   18 Hole Golf Course within 3 minutes walk of Hotel.

An advertising postcard from the Grand Marine Hotel, postmarked 1938.

The Golf Links, Barton on Sea

The following series of three photographs shows the evolution of Barton-on-Sea's golf links. This 1909 postcard of the Golf Links, Barton-on-Sea, shows the small club house.

Golf Club House, Barton-on-Sea.

The club house of the 1920s. Originally a nine-hole course in 1922, it was extended to a full course in 1932. Erosion has always caused problems for the club, and in the 1990s the course was finally relocated to land formerly belonging to Becton Farm.

THE CLUBHOUSE OF BARTON-ON-SEA GOLF CLUB
from which members enjoy unobstructed views of the Solent and Isle of Wight.

The bold Art Deco design of the new club house, built in the 1930s, remained until the move to Becton Farm.

'Thatched Cottage' on the corner of Grove Road and Dilly Lane is now a guest house, shown here in the snow in March 1917.

Durlston Court School in Becton Lane, Barton-on-Sea, in the late 1940s. The school was founded in Swanage, Dorset, in 1903 by Mr Atkinson, with Mr 'Pat' Cox as headmaster, a position he had held since 1926. Opened in 1909 in its present location by headmaster Mr Philip Stubbs, and originally known as 'Furzie Close', the buildings were taken over by Durlston Court School after the Second World War, having been temporarily relocated in Cumberland for the duration. Other local schools were relocated in wartime: Great Ballard Preparatory School to Stowell Park near Cheltenham, and Fernhill Manor boarding school, having been requisitioned by the authorities, to Stoke Abbott, Dorset, with the day school split between 'Henbury' in Mount Avenue, and Bashley Croft. In the same period, Homefield Preparatory School for Boys advertised 'Girls admitted for duration of war' and 'Good indoor air raid shelter'.

Westcliffe Buildings in Sea Road, Barton-on-Sea, in the 1950s, showing Sea Road Sub-Post Office in the centre of the building.

Right: Local lads pose for a photograph on the remains of an unknown ship wrecked at Chewton, said to have been carrying stone to Highcliffe Castle. Four of the lads are from the same family; Harold, Alec and Ben Plumley, with their cousin Jesse.

Below: The shipwreck of LT966, the *Berry Head*, at Steamer Point, Barton-on-Sea, in 1912. The boat was never re-floated and has disintegrated over the years.

six

South of the Town Centre

The Pantiles, photographed in 1956, showing Manns Brothers Ironmongers and their Vauxhall van with an advertising board fixed to its roof. The pumps, originally intended for petrol, were used to dispense paraffin and Esso Green TVO (tractor vaporising oil).

Opposite below: By the time this photograph was taken, in around 1940, Mann Bros had started selling National petrol from a roadside pump and sported a fine display of lawnmowers. The building on the road junction is the electricity company's showroom and offices.

Above: The Pantiles parade of shops in Lymington Road, built around 1908, looking towards Old Milton, *c.* 1920. The shop furthest from the camera is Mann Bros, a general hardware store, whose premises were used by Imperial and overseas troops while at Barton convalescent camp during the First World War. Next to Mann Bros is E.A. Stewart's tobacconist's shop where teas could also be purchased. The next shop along from Stewart's belongs to Miss Janet Bagshaw – a 'fancy needlework repository' according to the 1915 Kelly's Directory. The shop nearest to the camera is Mary's Tea Rooms owned by the Misses Corbett. Just visible, in the distance, are the infants' and juniors' schools on the junction of Lymington Road and Old Milton Road.

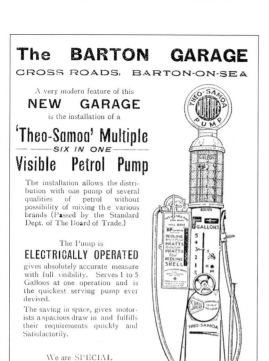

The BARTON GARAGE

CROSS ROADS, BARTON-ON-SEA

A very modern feature of this
NEW GARAGE
is the installation of a

'Theo-Samoa' Multiple
——SIX IN ONE——
Visible Petrol Pump

The installation allows the distri-
bution with one pump of several
qualities of petrol without
possibility of mixing the various
brands (Passed by the Standard
Dept. of The Board of Trade.)

The Pump is
ELECTRICALLY OPERATED
gives absolutely accurate measure
with full visibility. Serves 1 to 5
Gallons at one operation and is
the quickest serving pump ever
devised.

The saving in space, gives motor-
ists a spacious draw in and fulfills
their requirements quickly and
Satisfactorily.

We are SPECIAL
Austin Agents

and Visitors to the Garage will be
welcomed whether they are think-
ing of purchasing a new car or not
and details and demonstrations
given without obligation.

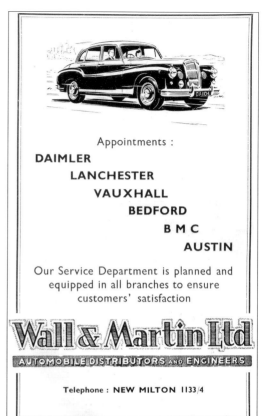

Appointments :
DAIMLER
LANCHESTER
VAUXHALL
BEDFORD
B M C
AUSTIN

Our Service Department is planned and
equipped in all branches to ensure
customers' satisfaction

Wall & Martin Ltd
AUTOMOBILE DISTRIBUTORS AND ENGINEERS

Telephone : NEW MILTON 1133/4

Above left: This 1930s advertisement from the *New Milton Advertiser* for the Barton Garage, on the corner of Lymington Road and Barton Court Avenue, shows the latest thing in petrol pumps. The garage was adapted for war work during the Second World War, repairing fighters. A local resident recalls, 'Aircraft on long low loaders, with wings off . . . being taken to and from the garage for repair'.

Above right: Wall & Martin Ltd, once the Barton Garage, had expanded their car dealership to six makes by the 1950s. The business was best known as a Vauxhall and Bedford main dealer and, although petrol is no longer sold, it is still a dealership today – the Olympian Renault showroom.

seven

North of the Town Centre

Ivy Bank, New Milton

The junction of Station Road and Manor Road. 'Ivybank', the house on the corner of Avenue Road on the left, is still there today – minus its balcony and distinctive spired tower.

The junction of Fernhill Lane and Manor Road, around 1915, showing (right to left): Herbert Edward Buchan (fruiterer), Horace A. Moody (draper), a greenhouse (owner unknown), A. Frampton (painter and ironmonger).

By the time this photograph was taken in 1934, C.R. Tarrant – Nurseyman & Seedsman – was occupying the whole block of shops with his Manor Road Nurseries. The fence and building on the right were to be demolished to make way for The Broadway parade of shops and businesses later in the 1930s.

New Milton Garage Ltd in Fernhill Lane, originally opened by Captain Roach in the 1920s, was owned by T.J. Pickworth in the 1930s. At this time Cooper's ran Central Garage in Whitefield Road and was a main dealer for Standard Cars. They later purchased New Milton Garage and the name was changed to Cooper's Garages Ltd. By 1950, the dealership had expanded to include Hillman, Standard and Rover. Charlie Earwicker, who served his apprenticeship there, is the young man in the photograph. The garage later went on to become the area's main Ford dealership before closing in August 1985.

Fernhill Lane, looking towards Bashley, around the beginning of the twentieth century. At this stage the Ballard stream flows across the road and a footbridge is provided for pedestrians.

From a postcard postmarked 1918, Fernhill Lane, looking towards New Milton with the water tower in the background. There is now a road bridge, although there is still a remnant of the watersplash to one side, and Fernhill Manor can be seen to the right. Documents for the Fernhill Estate go back to 1190. John Fromond gave the land to Winchester College, in 1420, to provide money from rents to pay for the clothing of sixteen choir boys. A couple of years after the arrival of the railway, the college began to sell parcels of land to developers. Miss Clarke and Miss Macnamara changed the name to Fernhill Manor in 1919, when they moved their Branksome Girls' College here. The college had been founded by Miss Hawkins in around 1893, occupying two locations near Ashley Arnewood, and was sold to Miss Clarke and Miss Macnamara in 1913. Fernhill Manor School recently closed and the buildings have now been converted to private housing.

An aerial photograph of Great Ballard in the early 1920s. Ballard Lake can be seen to the bottom right of the photograph, with Fernhill Lane just visible to the right, among the trees.

Great Ballard School in 1930. Originally the home of Colonel Ubsdell – Great Ballard became a preparatory school in 1924. The name was changed to Edinburgh House in 1945, then became part of Ballard Lake co-educational Preparatory School in 1995, merging with nearby Fernhill Manor Girls' School.

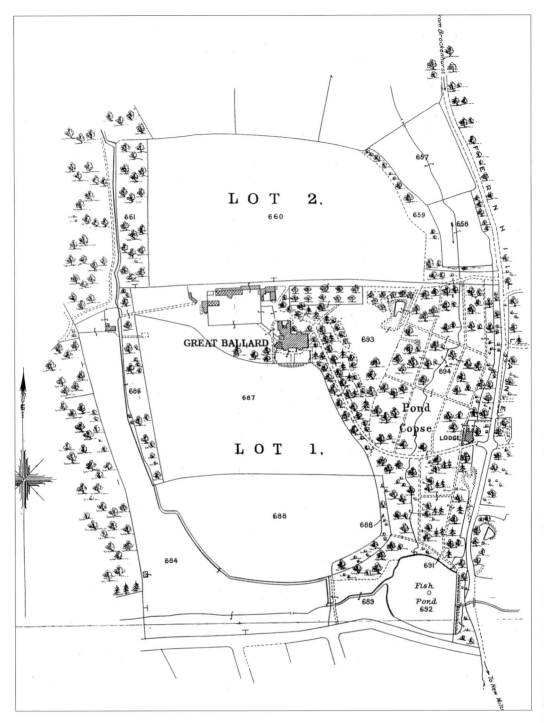

A plan of Great Ballard Estate, possibly from 1924 when Colonel Ubsdell sold the property, with the lake described as a 'fish pond'.

eight

Ashley

Ashley Road, looking towards New Milton, in the 1930s. Many of the private houses that lined Ashley Road were demolished to make way for flats.

Opposite: Originally thought to be a photograph of Litchford Hill, described in the 1910 Milton Ratepayers Association's official guide as 'Ashley Arnewood', it shows an unmade Ashley Road. The lack of traffic at this time is apparent from the people standing around in the road.

The bottom of Litchford Hill, in Ashley Road, looking towards Ashley. In the opposite direction, behind the camera, is a sharp left-hand bend. Author, Malcolm Bailey, remembers taking the corner at speed on a bicycle after school and nearly colliding with an oncoming car! The bend was later bypassed and the original road remains as a service road for bungalows.

An early view of Ashley Road, unmade and much narrower than today, looking from New Milton. Ashley Baptist Church and the crossroads are just visible in the background.

An aerial photograph of Ashley, in 1924, taken from the New Milton direction. Just visible at the bottom of the photograph is the bend in Ashley Road, at the bottom of Litchford Hill, with Ashley Crossroads near the top of the picture. The open fields on the right were later occupied by High Ridge Crescent, Ashley Secondary School (opened in 1939), Ashley sports ground, Molyneux Road and Ashley Parade.

Above: Ashley Road in the 1930s. The photograph shows Ashley Post Office on the right, owned by Bullock & Sons, and T.A. Molton's greengrocer's shop on the left – later taken over by the Bullock family. Prior to the opening of Ashley Post Office, mail had to be collected from the Royal Oak public house in Downton – where it had been delivered by the Lymington to Poole coach, for which a fee of 8*d* was levied. The first postmaster was William J. Talbot, who ran the bakery, while his wife Ethel managed the post office. The house and shop were built by Isaac Corbin, who lived there himself. William Talbot was replaced in 1906 by C. Morris who, in turn, was succeeded by Harry Bernard Burbidge in 1915. The next occupiers were Mr and Mrs Bullock, followed by Mr and Mrs Willams from Wales, then in 1972 by a keen opera singer with the Bournemouth Operatic Society named Denis Green.

Above: An aerial photograph, taken in 1945, of Ashley Secondary School. The school was opened in 1939 and later became Ashley Junior School. Just visible at the top left of the picture is High Ridge Crescent, built in the 1930s, where the school's headmaster – Mr W.R. Wakefield – later lived. Presumably he could keep an eye on things from there!

Opposite below: The back of the aerial photograph, of Ashley Secondary School, is signed by the seventeen teachers there in 1945. From the top: W.R. Wakefield (Headmaster), Miss E. Burgess (Senior Mistress & Mathematics), Tom Blaylock (Science), Elaine Jennings (Domestic Science), A.L.H. Ryall (Typing & Shorthand, also ran the Chess Club), W.H. Higgerson (General Subjects), E.J. Price (?), B.J. Isaacs(?), Miss D.L. Moss (General Studies), M.T. Perkins (?), Miss A.E. Troughton (General Studies), M.B. Lownes (?), Miss Holro (Art, originally taught Music), E.A. Williamson (?), R.H. Geenham (?), S.R. Wilkes (General Studies & Mathematics), K. Wakefield (School Secretary, also taught French). One of the school's best known characters is Arthur Lloyd, the history teacher from 10 October 1946 until 1970, when he moved to Arnewood School in Gore Road. Most pupils remember 'Tommy', as Arthur was known affectionately, and also recall his rhymes that were devised to help to remember historical facts. He is now well known as a local historian around the New Milton, Highcliffe and Lymington areas.

The area between New Milton and Ashley as seen from the air. The photograph is taken looking south, with Brook Avenue at the bottom of the picture, then Manor Road and the railway with the Solent and Isle of Wight in the distance. The greenhouses and surrounding fields, in the centre of the photograph, belonged to Stevenson's Nurseries. In 1926 Joe Stevenson purchased the market garden and copse on the north side of Ashley Road to the west of Ballard Stream, a total of thirty-two acres, from Frederick Peckham. This was a very modern market garden and pig farm with a superb thatch-covered piggery with about twenty sties. The glasshouses were modern and very productive. Joe Stevenson had built up a thriving business growing sweet peas when he started in commercial business after leaving his employment as head gardener to the Duke of Hamilton in 1907. The nursery was ideal for sweet peas with its pigsties and copse of hazel sticks. The nursery became famous for seed production, and hosted the National Sweet Pea Trials in 1931, when Joe Stevenson became President. In one period there were more than seven miles of sweet pea rows grown and this continued up to the Second World War. His two sons, Ronald and Hector, ran the nursery and were also very keen sportsmen. The family business is still prospering with nurseries in Gore Road, Pennington, Sussex and Devon, run by the fourth generation of Stevensons.

Above: Ashley Baptist Church was built in 1899 to replace the small chapel, further down Lower Ashley Road, next to the graveyard. The 1899 church was demolished to make way for a new building on 13 February 1993.

Left: J.R. Browning's grocery shop in Belmont Road. Admiring the jars of sweets in the window are the Corbin children: Victor, Kathleen, Mary, Clara and Minnie.

Opposite above: In 1934 William 'Bill' Bailey moved from Martin, near Fordingbridge, to Hordle after purchasing a small dairy business called Yeatton Dairy from Mr Fred Parker for £250. The business had one roundsman, Les Haynes, and eight gallons of milk a day was delivered using a motorcycle sidecar combination. A Singer van (pictured opposite) was purchased soon afterwards and was used to collect eggs from Ringwood market every Wednesday. Bill met Winifred Grant there and, in 1935, they married and moved into a bungalow in Sky End Lane. The dairy started to bottle milk and, to help with sales, an arrangement was made with The Beehive cake shop in Station Road to stock the dairy's milk in return for advertising space on milk bottles. Customers could also pay their milk bills at the shop, an arrangement that lasted the life of the dairy, from 1934 to 1961. The business continued to grow and, when the leases on both the dairy buildings and the bungalow expired in 1938, the business moved to larger premises in Ashley Common Road in Ashley. There was a house adjacent to the dairy, behind which there were some cows and chickens kept to supplement the supply of milk and eggs.

At the same time as the move to larger premises, the trading name of the business was changed to Hygienic Dairy. In 1939, output was up to 100 gallons a day and four horse-drawn milk floats were in use, as well as the Singer van. The horse-drawn milk floats were built locally by engineers, Cook & Sons at Old Milton, using a Ford 8 chassis. Butter, margarine and lard were bought in from Fairoak Dairy in Eastleigh.

During the Second World War butter was rationed to 2oz of butter, 2oz of margarine and 1oz of lard per customer. The area was 'zoned', as in other parts of the country, giving each dairy their own area to deliver milk in and taking away customer choice. The dairy started supplying milk to local schools in ⅓ pint bottles and opened a small shop at the Parkland caravan site selling milk, cream, butter, ice cream, cigarettes, sun hats and toys.

The business moved to larger premises in 1948, to Ashley Arnewood in Ashley Road – formerly a farm, as well as purchasing Manor Farm at Lymington for milk and egg production. An assortment of vehicles were used for deliveries, including Morrison electric floats, Morris J Series petrol floats, a Ford 8 van (a black one bought from a local undertaker!) and two horse-drawn floats. The horses, Trixie and Queenie, were pensioned off in 1955. As the dairy trade became less profitable, the business was sold to Edgar's Dairies on 30 March 1961, by which time the dairy was delivering 800 gallons of milk a day across thirteen milk rounds.

nine

Bashley, Wootton and Tiptoe

St John's Church in St John's Road, which was built in 1907, no longer has its own vicar. Instead it falls within the area covered by the rector of Milton Parish Church.

Bashley (sometimes known as Fernhill) crossroads as they were most probably in the 1930s. The farm buildings on the corner on the right were demolished to widen the junction. The house on the left belonged to Reg Fagan, the gents' outfitter in New Milton, in the 1950s.

This view showing the junction with Cull Lane and Sway Road, taken in 1908 from Mark's Lane, looks much the same today although this end of Cull Lane has been closed to traffic. The junction used to go by the colourful name of 'Pigsty Corner'.

The picturesque 'Willy's Well Tea Cottage', in Bashley Common Road near the Rising Sun Inn, in the early 1930s.

The Smithy in Bashley Cross Road in the 1920s. The last blacksmith to occupy the premises was Charles Loader. He was followed in 1947 by his son, Reginald Loader, who ran his engineering business there before moving to Bashley Road in 1951 to open Loader's Garage. The garage is still run by his son John today.

Bashley Post Office and General Store was opened in January 1902 – the first postmaster being Mr Albert Edward James. Postal services were good at this time, with two deliveries from New Milton on weekdays and one on Sundays. By 1933, the post office had closed, and was only opened again following a petition by the local Women's Institute. The post office reopened in 1935, under the management of Mr and Mrs Paul Platt, and continued to serve throughout the Second World War – surviving an air battle during which a German aircraft was shot down. The building was riddled with bullets, damaging books and grocery stock, although nobody was hurt as it was lunchtime and the shop was empty. Mr and Mrs William Fletcher took over the post office in the 1980s followed, in 1992, by Anthony Davies.

Veals' Corner at Bashley, shown here in the 1940s, was named after the Veal family whose cottage was on the bend to the right of this photograph. The corner has since been widened and smoothed.

ACCIDENT AT RISING SUN   26-8-38.

An accident outside the Rising Sun at Wootton, on 26 August 1938, involving a car driven by a Barton-on-Sea man and a milk lorry from Parkstone in Dorset. Seven people were involved in the accident including a female car passenger who suffered bruising to her forehead and right hand. The lorry, en route from Tiptoe to Holmsley, was in collision with the car that was being driven from New Milton towards Brockenhurst. The lorry, loaded with milk churns, overturned and (according to a report in the following week's *New Milton Advertiser*) 'milk was thrown all over the road'. The photograph shows the second Rising Sun – rebuilt in 1903.

Tiptoe Road, the heart of Wootton Village, near the beginning of the twentieth century. From the right are: Frank Soffe's bakery; the General Store, which was owned by Mrs Georgina C. Soffe in the 1920s/30s; the Primitive Methodist Chapel; the sub-post office just visible in the distance.

Georgina Soffe, with an assistant, standing in front of the General Store at Wootton.

Left: Wootton Sub-Post Office just as it was when Mrs Mary Ivemy took it over from her father in 1894. The sub-post office was opened in 1855 and was originally run by Mary's father, William Wallace. Later owners included Mr Harris from 1923, Miss Russell in the 1920s and Edmund James Wooldridge (father of the sports broadcaster Ian Wooldridge) from 1928. A new shop front was installed in 1937, with reconstruction of the house in 1939, following an unsuccessful attempt to sell the premises to the council for road widening. After the Second World War, the sub-post office and stores were run by W.S. Adams, then by D.G. Adams. At the time of its closure in 1973 the postmistress was Mrs Marches.

Below: The first Wootton School, in Tiptoe Road, was destroyed by lightning and the subsequent fire in 1914, and was rebuilt during the following year on the same site. This school, and the one that followed it, were both Church of England.
(F.J. Arnott, Lymington)

The second Wootton School, built in 1915, was a corrugated iron structure which lasted until the new school was built in 1936 – just across the boundary in Tiptoe village. At this time the school became non-denominational.

The pupils of Wootton School pictured, with the Headmaster Mr Coglan and Juniors Teacher Mrs Izzard, in the 1920s.

Above: Thomas Ackland's cottage at Tiptoe Cross which he built himself. From left to right are: daughters Rose and Nellie, wife Lucy and youngest daughter Louie. 'Tommy' Ackland was a well-known local wheelwright and carpenter who worked for A.T. Peterson during the building of Sway Tower. The tower was built during the period 1879-84 to demonstrate the strength of concrete and Tommy was responsible for the woodwork, as well as being the only worker to go right to the top of the 218ft tower to provide the finishing touches, for which he was paid £50.

Right: Thomas and Lucy (née Buckle) Ackland were married in Hordle. An accomplished carpenter, Tommy also worked for Lymington undertakers Diamond & Son, and built his own coffin prior to his death on 21 June 1933.

The centre of Tiptoe showing W.E. Haynes' garage. The house to the right of the garage, with the post box in front, became the post office when Wootton Post Office closed. Mrs Coombe was the postmistress. The post office later moved to the house on the left when Mr Alcorn became postmaster, once again run by a member of the Coombe family, where it remains to the present day.

An aerial view of Tiptoe from the south-east with Broadley House, built around 1900 by Mr Moser, in the foreground. Middle Road runs across the picture and Marley Mount can be seen in the top left corner.

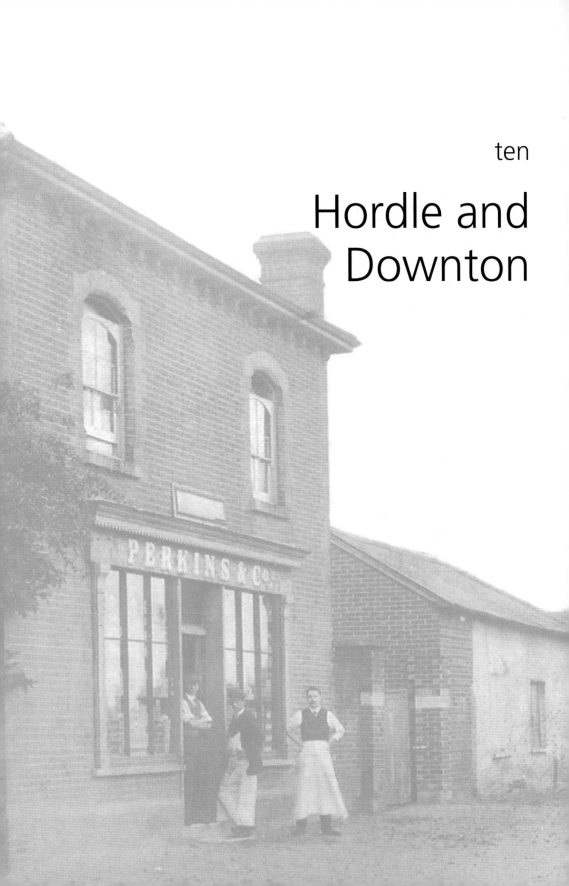

ten

Hordle and Downton

Although this postcard is entitled 'Golden Hill' it refers to the area. The view is of Hare Lane (looking towards Hordle). The postcard, postmarked 1914, was printed for H.B. Burbridge of Ashley Post Office and was addressed to: Mr Whitcher, 'Maycroft', Golden Hill, Hordle.

Lavender Farm Dairy was founded in the early 1930s by Herbert Bowring and his sons. Herbert had previously been the local postman. Supplying milk from their small herd of Guernsey cattle, the dairy started with a round of twenty-five customers – mostly in the Everton Road area of Hordle – dispensed from a can hung on the handlebars of a bicycle. When Herbert's sons left to serve in the Second World War, younger brother Roy joined the family business. Milk was still delivered by bicycle although, by this time, milk bottles with cardboard caps were in use. The dairy's first vehicle came into use in 1940/41. It was an Austin 7 van purchased from a butcher, John Robinson, in Ashley Common Road. Meanwhile, Lavender Farm took over the Hordle milk round of Lee Green Farm Dairy, whose business centred mainly on Milford-on-Sea. Roy Bowring Junior joined the business in the early 1970s. The business grew to ten milk rounds, accounting for around 5,000 customers in the early 1980s, although the impact of the large supermarkets has seen these figures drop to around 3,500 customers over recent years.

One of Lavender Farm Dairy's electric milk floats decorated for New Milton carnival in the 1980s. Nearest to the camera is Roy Bowring Junior's wife, Pat.

Hordle Radio & Electrical was started in 1947 by the partnership of Jim Bowman, Alfred 'Curly' Buckley and Tom Plummer, known locally as 'Pete'. The corrugated iron shops were built onto the front of Argyll House in Ashley Lane, then owned by Mr and Mrs Spreadbury, with the shop to the left occupied by fishmonger Fred Temple. The old shops were demolished in 1959 and new ones took their place. A smaller building to the right, which started off as a garage, was later converted to a launderette. In 1972 it became Hordle Electrical's offices. Originally the two sides of the business were electrical contracting and the retailing of radios – later branching out into television and domestic appliances. The firm's fleet of vehicles consisted of a Lanchester van and a motorcycle and later the two ex-GPO Morris 8 vans seen in the photograph above. Hordle Radio were also well known for television rentals, with 400 sets rented locally, although this side of the business was sold to Radio Rentals in the late 1970s. The proliferation of electrical superstores resulted in the retail side being closed down at this time. The business is now run by Geoff and Chris Plummer, and Bill Latimore, still concentrating on electrical contracting.

The original Three Bells public house at the Hordle end of Silver Street, which closed in the 1930s when the new pub was built near the Vaggs Lane junction.

Harry Perkins' shop in Everton Road with the bakery housed in the adjacent cob building. The cost to have ovens installed (on 16 March 1899) by Joseph Baker & Son of Willesden Junction, London, was £97 10s. The shop was later owned by grocers Alec Whitehead in the 1950s, when it was known as Central Stores, and by T. Gambrill in the 1960s.

The crossroads at Downton, on the Highcliffe to Lymington road, looking towards New Milton. The junction has changed dramatically since the photograph was taken with the demolition of the building on the left, and the wall near the road sign on the right, to allow for the straightening of the main road.

The Royal Oak public house was built in the eighteenth century and was well known as a staging post for the local area, for mail, for produce and supplies.

Downton had a post office as early as 1853 that was being managed by John Spracklen in 1855. Subsequent postmasters included George Wearn, the local blacksmith, in 1875; Elizabeth Wearn in June 1898; Miss Susan Ireland in 1899; Ellen Line in March 1909; Mrs E. Butler in 1911; Harry Hain in February 1912, succeeded by his wife Mary following his death around 1920, who continued until the business was sold in 1950. The post office finally closed in November 1979. To the right of the photograph, dairyman Louis Browning of Hordle is delivering milk, dispensed from a 15-gallon churn in his horse-drawn cart.

Ashley Clinton, with its distinctive observatory and water tower, was the home of Sir Henry Clinton from around 1800 until his death in 1829. The Clinton family were lords of the manor of Hordle from the mid-seventeenth century. The last of the Clinton line died in 1956 and the house has since been divided into separate dwellings. A 48-acre portion of the estate was purchased by the golf club at Barton-on-Sea, in the 1960s, to compensate for the loss of land due to cliff erosion.

eleven

People

Above: New Milton Council School football team in 1930. From left to right, back row: 'Skip' Barker, David Fry, 'Slug' Harman. Middle row: Frank Bennett, Don Browning, Ray Instell. Front row: Jim Oakley (or Sid Foster), Jim Bessant.

Left: A photograph of Charles Dallas, possibly taken outside his home in Eastley Wootton, in his 1899 25hp Lifu steam car – one of the first self-propelled vehicles in New Milton. The Lifu had a range of 60 miles at 12mph and carried 40 gallons of paraffin as well as 70 gallons of water. Charles Dallas' man-servant and companion, Jack Card, is seated in the back.

First Milton Scouts chopping wood behind the Rectory stables, at Old Milton, *c.* 1954. From left to right are: Mr Gibson's son, Mr Gibson (the probation officer for the area), 'Tubby' Prentiss (the current head of Holmfield School) and Michael Hodges.

The first Carnival Queen, with her attendants, and the British Legion Committee. From left to right, front row: ? Butcher, Violet Bessant, Ann Dyett, Joan Eagle, ? Butcher. Back row: Mr Eagle, Mr Rudkin, -?-, -?-, Mr Jones, -?-, Mr Uren. The photograph was taken in New Milton recreation ground, near the playground, *c.* 1933.

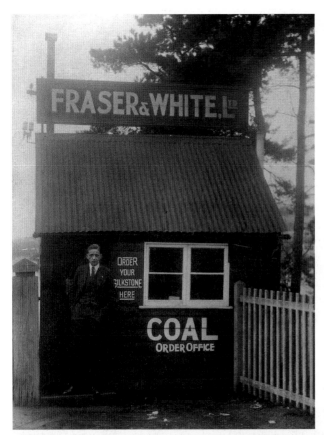

Left: James Bessant (husband of Violet Bessant), the manager of Fraser & White Ltd, standing outside their coal order office in the entrance to the station yard.

Below: Milton Pageant in 1920. The part of the 'knight on the horse' was played by George Gates.

Opposite above: Children celebrating VE Day at a party in the War Memorial Hall in Whitefield Road.

Above: The staff of Herbert H. Drew, building contractors, on a charabanc outing to Bath on 23 July 1921.

Overleaf: Dad's Army – the standing down parade of New Milton Home Guard on 12 December 1944. From left to right, back row: –?–, –?–, ? Jones, K. Powell, –?–, ? Ford-Horne, ? Renton, J. Corbin, –?–, N. Cato. Middle row: E. Major, J. Billing, –?–, –?–, ? Moore, C. Fry, G. Crowhurst, J. Boyce, J. Vicary, A.J. Whitcher. Front row: N. Gage, S. Hall, A. Cummings, W. Hasseldine, A. Dowland, –?–, W. Pitt, ? Harder (or Kitcher), Col. Kirby (?), W. Horsford, S. Whitcher, ? Edwards, ? Ireland, ? Goodyer.

Hygienic Dairy's wartime staff. In 1941 the three roundsmen – Les Haines, Eddie Rouse and Les Warren – were called up for National Service and Land Army girls were brought in to take their place. Back row, from left: Bill Bailey, Winifred Bailey, Reg Tuckerman (dairy manager), 'Jimmy', Eileen Keats, Michael Rickman. Front row: Vera Thorpe, Lucy Merryfield, Belinda Powell, Olive Breaker, Phyllis Skew.

The Corbins, a well-known local family, pictured in 1925. From left to right are: Herbert, Dorothy, Rose and Dorothy's mother, Winifred.

New Milton's hand pump, on 'active' duty, with the fire crew giving a demonstration at New Milton Fête on the recreation ground in the 1950s. The hand pump, built in 1897, came from Lymington Fire Brigade to New Milton in 1919 and is now fully restored and kept in the current fire station on the corner of Whitefield Road.

The end of the road for an old Ford, used for the last time by New Milton's firemen, in the carnival in the 1950s. From left to right are: John Hutchins, Joe Everett, Bert Skew, Geoffrey Batchelor, Terry Bailey, Bob Adams. The boy's name is not known although he may have been the son of one of the firemen.

Acknowledgements

We are indebted to the following people, without whom this book could not have been written, for their contribution of photographs and information:

Mrs Winifred Bailey, Mrs Violet Bessant, Mr Roy Bowring, Mr Tony Cook, Mrs Audrey Corbin & family, Mrs Rosemary Courtney, Mr Eddie Curry, Mrs Gill Doran, Mr Ben Earwicker, Mr Charlie Earwicker, Mr Robert Fagan, Mr Roy Fulford, Mr Vernon Gates, Rob & Kath Goodacre, Miss Rachel Hickman, Mr Michael Hodges, Hordle Radio & Electrical Ltd, Mr John Hutchins, Mr Jude James, Mrs Dorothy Johnson, Mr Arthur Lloyd, Mr Jim Lush, Mr Carl Mondz, Mr Alan Selby, Mr Wilf Simpkins, Smith & Son Printers, Mr Hugh Stevenson, Mr George Stickland, Mr M.C. Taylor.

Thanks are also due to the *New Milton Advertiser & Lymington Times* and St Barbe Museum & Art Gallery.